A Journey
Back
to Me

A Journey Back to Me

Rediscovering Physical, Emotional, and Spiritual Wholeness

ConSandra Jones

A Journey Back to Me: Rediscovering Physical, Emotional, and Spiritual Wholeness
Whole Person Journey Series, Book 1
ISBN 0-9676490-3-X

Second Edition

Published by Koinonia Publishing
P.O. Box 542021
Houston, Texas 77254-2021

Library of Congress Card Number: 99-091711

Cover Design by Sachnowitz & Co.
Author's Photograph by Gittings & Lorfing
Interior Production by Mustard Seed Studio, Inc.
Edited by Judy King

Self-Improvement. Self-Care. Recovery. Inspirational.

DEDICATION

This book is dedicated to the Joy of my Journey,
Davi and Dannin.

This book is also dedicated to the memory of my daddy,
Curtis, who taught me about Jesus, my Heavenly Father, and
insisted that I prepare to be independent.

Thank you, Daddy, for being who you were, who dreamed
more for me than I could imagine, who realized my potential
decades before I knew I had potential. Thank you for being there
with me and for me!

I miss you. How I wish you could be here to share my life
with all its peaks and valleys. I want to smell, touch, and feel
you. I know you're watching; I just wish I could see you. Now I
realize how much my relationship with you shapes how I relate to
others. I am truly grateful that you modeled Christ for me.

Thank you for teaching me how to live and love just as Christ
has taught us—to love unconditionally.

I love you.

CONTENTS

Acknowledgments

Foreword

Preface

Part I: The Awakening

Part II: The Journey

Part III: Restoration

ACKNOWLEDGMENTS

I must acknowledge and openly appreciate my support system:

To the Trinity—the Father, the Son, and the Holy Ghost—who made me and this book possible—I love, worship, and adore you!

To my parents, Curtis Earl and Dossie Mae Jones—Thank you for raising me in the Christian faith, teaching me, and being there for me. I am truly grateful for your love and guidance.

To my pastors, the late Rev. J. G. Russ and Pastor A. L. Patterson, for giving me a firm Christian foundation. And to Pastor Ralph Douglas West for washing and nurturing me in the Word, also for being a friend who was there when I needed you—you are the epitome of a teacher and friend.

To my family and friends who have been there for me and prayed with me as I've gone through bumps and bruises especially since 1990. I love and appreciate you.

To Jennifer Agnew Scott and Dawn Cherie Kennedy, my cheerleaders and the voices of accountability for finally birthing this book.

To Jerry Boles, Jeanne Dorsey, Dennis and Diana Harris, Diane Sams, and Ken Sams who helped me endure through the toughest time of my life—thanks for being there for me.

And to my extended family of Brookhollow Baptist Church, The Church Without Walls—how I thank God for the love and support He has provided through each of you.

FOREWORD

...*"After you have suffered a little while, will (Christ) himself restore you and make you strong, firm and steadfast."*
—*1 Peter 5:10*

I have known ConSandra Jones for several years and have been privy, as her pastor, to much of what she has experienced, so I was not surprised to learn that she was writing a book. There are those lives that demand documentation, examination, and sharing. Her life is one of those.

This is an intensely personal book. I have read a lot of books written by women. It is noteworthy that most women do not write for money or recognition. They usually write to maintain emotional, intellectual, and spiritual clarity and to sustain self-development and instruction. ConSandra is not an exception.

This book offers a wonderful opportunity for you to journey through self-awareness, self-discovery and to arrive at some trans-forming junctions of your own life. The journey to achieving wholeness is not an easy one, yet the rewards are well worth the price. I recommend this book to all who need or desire restoration.

I hope many say "yes" to *A Journey Back to Me.*

Ralph Douglas West
Pastor/Founder
The Church Without Walls

PREFACE

I invite you to take a journey with me. It is my journey of faith, through healing to renewal and restoration. As in most travel experiences, you should expect the unexpected. Have no fear; you are simply along for the ride. As we take this journey, I'll relate some experiences to Biblical principles. I trust that this journey will bless the lives of you who are seeking wholeness.

I'm sure you have your own travel routine. Sit back and relax; you are with an experienced traveler. I know how to read a road map, follow detour signs, and find my way through unfamiliar territory, yet I will readily admit that this journey is different from any other.

I think it's only fair to warn you that we'll start out in some inclement conditions; get ready for some turbulence. We'll encounter some battles and storms. Be prepared to see me stripped, robbed, and beaten. There are times when I will be misunderstood. We could possibly lose our way. Just when you think you know where we're headed, expect some detours. If we get caught in quicksand, we'll get out when the time is right. You may see some situations you can identify with. There will be times when we cannot see what is right in front of us. Remember, we are going through!

By the time this journey ends, I'll find out who I really am and what I am made of. And you may become curious enough to begin your own exploration.

As your navigator, I'll teach you to recognize what is happening in the spiritual realm, not just in the physical realm. You will learn the importance of faith and perseverance to endure to your ultimate destination. You will learn the importance of taking care of yourself—physically, emotionally, and spiritually. You will recognize that you are never alone in the challenges you face. And you will see that you and God can make it through anything!

Just read along, observe and learn as much as you can as we travel this journey back to me. Rest assured we'll finish exactly where we are supposed to be!

I

The Awakening

CHAPTER 1

The Journey
Begins...

I wrote this letter to my husband almost three years before I started writing this book:

September 1995

This letter is an attempt to communicate with you in a way that I haven't in some time. It is the only way I can totally open up to you. I feel compelled to, at this point, because I have not had the opportunity lately. It is probably more beneficial to me than to you, however, I'm sure you'll find it enlightening.

During the past six to eight weeks, my life has been in swift transition. There were major decisions to face regarding our lives together and my life individually—with you, employment and car decisions; for me, business and health decisions; for our children, individual best interest and school-related decisions. The decisions were made; I have dealt with them by being Spirit-led. And I believe that they have been made in the best interest of our family.

Since August 27, the day Pastor West preached the sermon, "Do You Really Want to Be Made Well?", I have been on a journey, one which I rarely allow myself to take—a journey both for and about me. By divine coincidence, I started reading Ordering Your Private World _August 1, and I immediately began reorganizing my thoughts, then I began physically reorganizing my life. Since August 27 I have recommitted to doing whatever it takes to become well again. When I say well, I don't mean just physically—I mean experiencing a wholeness that only Jesus can facilitate. What I have realized is I can only_ be who I am, and when I do more than that, I become frustrated and confused. I finally understand what I need. I need someone who, more than anything else and before anything else, loves me the way I need to be loved—totally and unconditionally. And I must have that to be WHOLE AGAIN!!!

In my journey to wholeness, I have declared my independence from everyone except Jesus because He is the only one who can give me all that I need. This process began in 1990, and today it has grown to a different level.

I know that this is in preparation for something. I can only speculate what it is in preparation for, but I do know that when the Lord knows I'm ready, He'll show me. I can't find wholeness in being who you want me to be or what I want to be, which is to simply be happy and have peace in my life. Wholeness will come when I have fulfilled what it is Jesus has for me.

The endoscopy a couple of weeks ago is a part of the journey; it was a diagnosis of what was going on internally, physically and mentally. I still had a small portion of the ulcer that needed treatment and that's what I'm doing these days . . . doing all that I can do to encourage healing—spiritually, physically, and emotionally. I have issues that need to be resolved; I'm working on them. And as I told you a few weeks ago, I intend to do whatever it takes to get well!

I trust that this will help you understand me.

CHAPTER 2

*Uncovering
the
Issues*

ach of us has issues. They may differ in size, range, or depth, but they are indeed our issues. They either have originated from our childhood or developed during our adulthood. They may be short- or long-term. These issues may be emotional, physical, or spiritual or a combination thereof.

In 1994 I collapsed and almost died from two bleeding ulcers—I had issues. As I was rushed to the doctor and then to the hospital, it felt as though I were living a nightmare. My four-year-old son was with me. He watched as I vomited blood, collapsed, and was driven home. While I waited for my husband to arrive at home, my son took care of me. I wondered what kind of effect the incident would have on him. I saw fear in his face and tears in his eyes, yet he never seemed overwhelmed. It was the scariest day of our lives. We started off that morning on the way to school and ended up in the hospital intensive care unit.

As I lay in the hospital bed facing some very real issues, I reflected on my priorities, my problems, and my plans. I realized that I wanted to live life my way, the way which had landed me in this precarious condition. I knew that I was much closer to death than life. I had two children to raise, and I asked the Lord for my life so I could raise them His way. I knew that I had to make some drastic changes in my life. Only later would I discover how difficult the decisions for change would become.

After I was released from the hospital and was recovering at home, I reflected on the illness, the incident, and my issues. I wanted to get well. I followed doctors' orders, took the medication as directed, changed my diet, and got plenty of rest. Six weeks later when I went for a follow-up visit with the doctor, only one of the ulcers had healed. The doctor was surprised; he said both ulcers should have healed. Evidently it was going to take a little longer for the complete healing to occur.

Over the next year and a half we wrestled with that ulcer which should have healed within that first six-week period. My doctors prescribed stress management, counseling, different prescriptions, a bland diet, and more rest. Each time I was evaluated, the results were the same—the ulcer (issue) prevailed. Eventually my doctors became alarmed; I was a young woman with an ulcer that would not heal and a family history of cancer.

The gastroenterologist recommended that I have another test. *I refused*—I knew the ulcer had not healed. There was no point in allowing him to insert a tube down my throat to my stomach to tell me what I already knew—*the ulcer was still there.* I had been tested four times since my hospitalization. To avoid liability, the doctor sent a letter to document that I had not followed his recommendation. In the meantime I sought the second opinion of another specialist. He agreed with the first doctor. I was at high risk for stomach cancer, and they both recommended surgery. Again I refused. Next I visited a third doctor for an opinion and shared the history of this ulcer. He agreed with the previous doctors, yet he prescribed a different medication, his final recommendation before requiring surgery. He said that "it was what he would do for his mother" if she were in my situation. I was ecstatic to find any option. I had the prescription filled and began to work together with God for my healing.

During that summer my pastor, Ralph Douglas West of Brookhollow Baptist Church, The Church Without Walls, in Houston, Texas, had preached a sermon entitled "Do You Really Want to Be Made Well?", based on the following scripture:

Some time later, Jesus went up to Jerusalem for a feast of the Jews. Now there is in Jerusalem near the Sheep Gate a pool, which in Aramaic is called Bethesda and which is surrounded by five covered colonnades. Here a great number of disabled people used to lie—the blind, the lame, the paralyzed. One who was there had been an invalid for thirty-eight years. When Jesus saw him lying there and learned that he had been in this condition for a long time, he asked him, "Do you want to get well?"

"Sir," the invalid replied, "I have no one to help me into the pool when the water is stirred. While I am trying to get in, someone else goes down ahead of me."

Then Jesus said to him, "Get up! Pick up your mat and walk." At once the man was cured; he picked up his mat and walked. —John 5:1-9

Pastor West challenged us, "Do you want to be well in spite of your hopelessness? . . . You can be spiritually well if you seize the moment of opportunity, and trust God to get you off your mat!" He reminded us, "In the midst of your routine faithfulness, the extraordinary can occur if we are willing to seize the moment." That sermon transformed my desire into action! I was ready and willing to seize the moment. More than anything, I wanted to become well, not only spiritually, but physically and emotionally. I became committed to doing everything I could to get well. I was a workaholic, so instead of working 60 hours each week, I worked 25 to 30 hours. I completely changed my diet. And I began reading, listening, and meditating on God's Word daily. The Lord began a mighty work in me. And I surrendered my life to allow Him to complete the healing within me.

We, the Lord and I, began to clean some things up. I made some life-changing decisions, altered my physical and spiritual diet, and began reconditioning my mind. I started each day with Him in meditation, prayer, and Bible study. I took a spiritual and holistic approach to healing by eliminating meat from my diet and eating mostly fruits and vegetables. Then I began evaluating the things that caused stress in my life. I realized that I had to reorganize to make me important again. I was so busy taking care of my husband, my children, and my business that I didn't have anything left for me. I had two young children. I had founded and was managing a staffing firm that was growing rapidly. And I had a husband who was focused on himself and his view of success. I was frustrated, angry, and disappointed. I felt like I was juggling everything alone.

A few months before I collapsed from the ulcers, I had a car accident. A car ran a red light and hit my car on the driver's side. Had our cars collided a couple of inches closer to the driver's seat, I would have been dead. The accident shook me up physically and emotionally. These things were not supposed to be happening to me. As I reflected on my life, I asked, "Am I happy? Am I content? Where is my peace? Why do I feel that I am raising the children alone? Are my needs being met? Am I living a life that is pleasing to God? Am I fulfilling His will for my life? Am I glorifying Him?"

I recognized that I was taking care of everyone's needs except my own.

We do not arrive at the point of desperation on our own. Or do we? Had I? Today we have monumental tasks at hand. Our families, our jobs, and our relationships require most of our attention. By evening when it's time to wind down, we have nothing left to give to ourselves. And what we usually fail to remember is that in order to love others, we must first like, love, and take care of ourselves.

Loving yourself means taking care of yourself. If you have children, you can recall what it was like when you brought that first baby home—you wanted to provide for its every need.

You nurtured it during pregnancy, labored through its delivery, and then it was time to get to know one another personally. You cradled that baby in your arms, cuddled it, kissed it, and tried to give it all that it needed. This is how your new love for yourself should begin. We take care of our "babies" (whether they are infants, relationships, or special projects) much better than we take care of ourselves.

We must begin by loving ourselves, doing things for ourselves, and taking care of ourselves. We easily fall into the habit of pleasing and doing for others while forgetting about ourselves. After a while, it becomes very frustrating to watch everyone else getting his needs met while we are empty because we are not nurtured. What does this have to do with dealing with issues? EVERYTHING! All healing begins within us!

We are the glue that holds our lives and families together. But who and what holds us together? Have we scheduled maintenance for our physical, spiritual, and emotional needs? Or do we just run until we need repair? Are we allowing ourselves to run out of the fuel we need to endure?

What do you do for you? Do you get a massage, listen to music, play a recreational sport, have dinner with a friend, go to the movies, work out, or have a weekend getaway? Do you buy yourself fresh flowers? Do you ever take time to walk and observe the beauty around you or simply relax in the stillness of candlelight and a bubble bath? One of my favorite treats is to check into a hotel alone and read or take time to reflect on what is happening in my life. I order room service and pamper myself until I check out.

If we are not taking care of ourselves, we are letting our lives control us. When we take proper care of ourselves, we eat healthy—for example, eat plenty of fruits and vegetables, forget fried foods, and drink lots of water. Taking care of ourselves also includes exercising regularly which helps clear our minds and our bodies of the toxins we take in. Get plenty of rest; don't feel guilty for taking the time just to relax. It's good for the mind, body, and soul. In addition, help your body to rejuvenate by getting at least nine hours of sleep each night. Empower yourself by studying and meditating daily on that which helps bring order into your life. I recommend God's Word. Laugh; it's nature's medicine to heal the mind and soul. And find something you enjoy doing and do it—we need to take time to nurture ourselves, whether it is reading, watching or playing a recreational sport, or just listening to music. Rest. Relax. Nurture yourself. _Take control of your life. Take care of yourself. Begin today!_

This journey is about dealing with our issues, becoming whole, helping bring forth our deliverance and examining our faith—the faith that allows God to change our attitudes about our circumstances. As an African-American woman, I realize that it is often difficult for many women to share our experiences with others. _I suffered alone._ I did not believe that my trials were anyone else's business. I did not want to bother anyone; they had their own lives and challenges. I was embarrassed and felt that the challenges I experienced were happening only to me. Please know, it is not just you who is suffering and it wasn't just me. We are all in this together. This book is written to dispel those myths because we need to share our trials and our triumphs. I want you to recognize that there is nothing wrong with having issues. It's natural; we all have them. Some are bigger than others. Our responsibility is to work through the issues and *become the whole person that we are designed to be.*

It is through sharing that we can help deliver others in bondage from their issues. When we share our lives with one another, we find that others have experienced some of the same challenges we have. Once we start talking about our struggles and challenges, we'll find encouragement that we can make it through life's battles. As we experience our wholeness, we must share our stories with others—believe me, others are desperately waiting for a breakthrough!

CHAPTER 3

*Desperation—
The Fork
in the Road*

IN MARRIAGE

*U*ntil age 30 I had lived what I considered to be a relatively normal life. I grew up in a rural town in Arkansas and married my high-school sweetheart at the age of 20. We moved to Houston and began to live the American dream. He had started a retail career about age 14; by the time we married, he was in middle management. I completed my undergraduate degree after we were married. By that time he had become vice president of a manufacturing company, which allowed us some symbols of success—a beautiful home, nice car, and a comfortable living. His goal was to become a self-employed millionaire, so when things started changing in corporate America, he decided to start his own wholesale clothing firm. This firm was the first of many entrepreneurial ventures throughout a seven-year period. The business ventures started off successful, but they failed to sustain. The roller coaster ventures eventually took a tremendous toll on our marriage.

After five years of marriage, we had a beautiful daughter. Once when I hired a sitter, the sitter said to me, "You all live like the Huxtables." The Huxtables were a successful African-American family whom most of America visited weekly in the '80s. *The Cosby Show* was a television sitcom starring Bill Cosby and Phylicia Rashad, a doctor and an attorney respectively. The comedy illustrated the daily lives of this atypical African-American family with their very typical problems. We were actually nothing like the Huxtables. Her comment was

ironic. She observed our life after a business deal had gone
bad—we lost a house and a couple of cars, and had mounting
debt. She said this while we were living in a rented home which
was considerably more modest than the homes we had previously
owned or rented. It became clear to me at that point that what
people saw and what was reality were two distinctly different
scenarios. In fact, our life was the opposite of what it appeared
to be.

By the time I was pregnant with our second child, I realized
that I was married to a man whom I loved but with whom I knew
I could not spend the rest of my life. We were unevenly yoked
and miserable. The quest for success at any cost, the decisions
to sacrifice everything in order to have what success looks like
had left me bitter and empty. I had married someone whose
definition of success and happiness was very different from mine.
To outsiders, we looked like the perfect couple, but inside the
marriage there was tension, disappointment, and frustration. It
took several years and a couple of brushes with death to jolt me
into reality. I wanted my children to have the life I had, growing
up in a home with two loving parents. I was carrying the family
emotionally and spiritually. I knew it was not God's will that
we divorce. I also knew our family was not experiencing *the
abundant life*. I was not living the life that God had created
me to live.

*I am come that they might have life, and that they might have
it more abundantly.* —John 10:10 (King James Version)

I felt trapped in the marriage. I was unhappy, but I didn't want to leave. We were miserable. I had given everything I could give, but I didn't know whether it was enough. I had been praying about our marriage for years, continuing because I did not want to be out of the will of God. As a Christian, I know God hates divorce. However, I didn't believe He wanted me to live in this chaotic, confused, and broken situation. I wanted to stay for the kids, but the daily struggle was draining everything from me.

That summer I had taken the children to my mother for their annual visit. As I sat on her porch questioning whether I had the strength to get up and try the marriage again, I was punch-drunk from the years of battling with decisions, made on my behalf, that felt wrong. I realized that the faith I should have had in God had been misplaced in a man whom I so desperately wanted to believe. He said that he was making the best decisions for us, but I realized after many years that he was not yielding to the authority or guidance of our Heavenly Father, so he was not deciding what was best for me.

Our daughter was six years old; our son was two years old. Both were our lifelines; they were a perfect blend of the two of us. But were the children enough to keep us committed to a marriage that was not working? By this time many things had happened—businesses had come and gone, material things had come and gone, and our youth it seemed had come and gone. We both loved the children, but our relationship had been lost in the midst of pain and disappointment. Could we hang in there until things got better? Would things get better?

I remember saying to my mother, "I don't think I can go back again." She looked at me and said, "You have to." I cried the entire six-hour drive back to Houston. During the drive back I bought a soundtrack by Tina Turner and played "I Don't Really Wanna Fight No More" over and over and over again. The lyrics said exactly what I felt.

When I returned to Houston, I remember sitting at the table with my husband and listening to him say, "I'm glad you came back." We both knew the past months had been hell and we both had been trying to survive until summer when we could take a break without the kids to see if there was anything left to build on. Although we were very successful early in our marriage, now each day was a struggle emotionally and financially. I had no idea of the tremendous toll it was taking on me physically.

I've never been a coward, but I wasn't at all sure I had what it took to make it without a partner. I had been with this man all my adult life. What I didn't realize was that my greatest strength and true partner had been there all my life. I was so busy focusing on the physical partner that I had forgotten about my spiritual partner. I did not think about how dependable and loyal Jesus is. He was there when I lost my father, and every time I needed Him. How did I overlook Him? He had provided all that I needed each time I needed it, yet I kept looking to my husband to provide the support and security I wanted. I began to wonder how I was going to make it. . . . I was scared.

IN HEALTH

It is amazing how stress affects our bodies. For several years I had been experiencing various health problems—headaches, digestive disorders, and gynecological problems. For years I did not make the connection; I later realized that each condition was brought on by stress.

By April of 1994 I had severe gynecological problems. I needed diagnostic surgery to confirm my condition, and after two years I finally was brave enough to have the surgery. The week before my surgery was scheduled, my husband asked me to reschedule the operation because he wanted to go to Washington, DC to meet some people before one of his friends left there to relocate to Houston. Once again he put his agenda ahead of my needs. He wasn't going to close a deal, just to network. He expected me to reschedule the surgery I had been afraid of in order to accommodate his trip. Would I take the back seat again? He ignored the fact that it had taken years for me to gather the courage for the surgery. Would I accept that once again my needs were being ignored? I didn't change my plans. He went to DC, and my mother came to Houston to take care of the kids and I. A friend picked her up when she arrived in the middle of the night; another friend drove us to the hospital, stayed there during the surgery, and took us home afterwards. My husband never apologized, and when he returned to Houston, he was angry that I had not changed my plans to fit his schedule. This incident marked the beginning of the end of our marriage.

When this happened, I realized that my husband's agenda took precedence over everything, including my well-being. I knew that I needed to get out of the back seat and prepare to become a single parent. Although I had some career experience, our focus had always been his career. Once the children came, my primary focus was taking care of them and I chose to put my career on hold. I had founded a temporary staffing firm; it was supposed to be a way to generate an income while maintaining my flexibility for the children. As a soon-to-become-single parent, I knew that I needed to prepare financially for my children. I began to work 60-hour weeks to establish the business. I was committed to positioning myself and my children financially for life.

In July of 1994 a car ran a red light and hit me; it was purely by God's grace that I survived. The car hit me on the driver's side, inches from where I was sitting. Since then my life has not been the same. I lost some memory as well as my sense of smell and taste. It has taken me years to recover physically and mentally. The impact of the crash was so severe that it caused my teeth to shift.

Finally in September of 1994 I collapsed with two bleeding ulcers and nearly died. I was admitted into the hospital intensive care unit, where I received a transfusion of two pints of blood. My son was with me and experienced the entire traumatic event as I passed out, hemorrhaged, and went in and out of consciousness while being rushed to the hospital. Although he was four years old when it happened, today he continues to talk to me about the incident.

As I lay in the hospital fighting for my life, I asked the Lord to let me live to take care of my children. I knew I had to survive for them. Unfortunately their father had demonstrated time and time again that he was not capable of focusing on anyone's needs other than his own. My brush with death scared him enough to begin to try to make me a priority in his life, but I was only a temporary priority. One and a half years later when I was still battling with one of the ulcers and he was trying to take the business, I realized that the only way I was to get rid of the ulcer was to deal with the issues in my marriage. When I told my doctor what the source of the problem was, he could not believe that I was speaking of the person he knew.

By this time I had come full circle—I had been me, I had been who my husband wanted me to be, and nothing was enough for him. I realized that nothing I did would ever be enough. There would not ever be enough money, clout, anything. The marriage was over, and all I wanted was to stop the merry-go-round and get off.

I share the details of my marriage to illustrate how issues control our lives. When our issues bring us to a point of death—physical, emotional, or spiritual—we must take control of our own destiny. We can rise to the challenge or let them kill us. My issues may not be your issues, but the steps to recovery are the same. More than anything, I want you to learn how to recover and to become restored. The process is not finished until we have healed enough to help others. Years ago when African-American slaves were set free, it was not freedom when a few slaves were independent. Freedom occurs when people, as a whole, are liberated from that which entangles them. I trust that by sharing my experiences with you, you also will discover your freedom!

CHAPTER 4

Discovering
Your
Faith

*A*s people of the new millennium, we are faced with challenges like never before. The demographics of society have changed from a male-dominated society to a society where women play an increasingly important role. We are mothers, CEOs, presidents, corporate officers, heads of households, pastors, deans, attorneys, and political representatives. We are decision makers; we are leaders. As our roles have evolved, so have the challenges that accompany these progressive roles. We find that in many cases women have become the point person for our families. We are family leaders, and we must realize that our children's destinies lie in our hands. We should position ourselves and our families for success—spiritually, emotionally, and physically. What we teach our children will determine what life is like for the next generation. Our task is monumental, yet we know we can handle anything with God by our side watching and guiding us. He is our Father. We must have faith in Him. We must have faith in ourselves. If we give Him the position, authority, and leadership in our lives, our families can be all He wants them to be.

When Jesus had again crossed over by boat to the other side of the lake, a large crowd gathered around him while he was by the lake. Then one of the synagogue rulers, named Jairus, came there. Seeing Jesus, he fell at his feet and pleaded earnestly with him, "My little daughter is dying. Please come and put your hands on her so that she will be healed and live." So Jesus went with him.

A large crowd followed and pressed around him. And a woman was there who had been subject to bleeding for twelve years. She had suffered a great deal under the care of many doctors and spent all she had, yet instead of getting better she grew worse. When she heard about Jesus, she came up behind him in the crowd and touched his cloak, because she thought, "If I just touch his clothes, I will be healed." Immediately her bleeding stopped and she felt in her body that she was freed from her suffering.

At once Jesus realized that power had gone out from him. He turned around in the crowd and asked, "Who touched my clothes?"

"You see the people crowding against you," his disciples answered, "and yet you can ask, 'Who touched me?'" But Jesus kept looking around to see who had done it. Then the woman, knowing what had happened to her, came and fell at his feet and, trembling with fear, told him the whole truth. He said to her, "Daughter, your faith has healed you. Go in peace and be freed from your suffering."

While Jesus was still speaking, some men came from the house of Jairus, the synagogue ruler. "Your daughter is dead," they said. "Why bother the teacher any more?"

Ignoring what they said, Jesus told the synagogue ruler, "Don't be afraid; just believe."

He did not let anyone follow him except Peter, James and

John the brother of James. When they came to the home of the synagogue ruler, Jesus saw a commotion, with people crying and wailing loudly. He went in and said to them, "Why all this commotion and wailing? The child is not dead but asleep." But they laughed at him.

After he put them all out, he took the child's father and mother and the disciples who were with him, and went where the child was. He took her by the hand and said to her, "Talitha koum!" (which means, "Little girl, I say to you, get up!"). Immediately the girl stood up and walked around (she was twelve years old). At this they were completely astonished. He gave strict orders not to let anyone know about this, and told them to give her something to eat. — Mark 5:21-43

This scripture is the foundation of this book. I'll refer to different passages throughout our journey.

The events in this scripture are about faith. The story about the woman with the issue of blood is neatly tucked within another story about restoration. It begins with Jairus and his daughter, stops abruptly, tells of the woman with the issue of blood, then immediately picks up where it left off with Jairus. Both passages are about people dealing with issues. They illustrate that in order for us to begin our restoration, we must first deal with our issues. However, we must realize that both _the resolution of issues and the restoration process are based on our faith._ **Jesus told the**

woman her faith had healed her; he told Jairus not to be afraid, just believe.

Faith is what we believe in spite of what we can see. Our faith motivates us to take action in bringing forth our healing; it doesn't automatically happen. *Sometimes we must believe it, feel it, know it, and act on it before our deliverance can come!*

As Jesus affirmed the healing of the woman with the issue of blood, some of Jairus' men came for Him. Jesus comforted Jairus by telling him not to be afraid, only to believe. This child was his future; everything he hoped for lay dormant before him. He was a dignified synagogue ruler and a leader in his community. He was probably accustomed to people coming to him for assistance, not seeking others to do for him what he could not do for himself. This was a man in need. Men by their very nature are proud and typically don't surrender to emotion as women do. Jairus laid aside his pride because the Word says, *"He fell at his* (Jesus') *feet and pleaded earnestly."* In the story it appears that his daughter's death occurred quickly. It brought him to a point of desperation!

Jesus requires that we believe in Him. He told the woman with the issue of blood that she had been healed because of her faith. He told Jairus to believe. As He approached Jairus' home where the girl lay, He did not allow any of the crowd to follow Him because they did not believe. Peter, James, and John were with Him; they saw the professional mourners who had been hired, according to the custom of the time, to dramatize this tragedy. When He said the child was asleep, the crowd laughed. Jesus, his companions, Jairus, and the child's mother entered the room where the child lay sleeping. Jesus awakened her; she stood up and walked around. She was revived and restored because her father, Jairus, **believed**. His faith brought her back to life!

A Woman with an Issue

A large crowd followed and pressed around him. And a woman was there who had been subject to bleeding for twelve years. She had suffered a great deal under the care of many doctors and spent all she had, yet instead of getting better she grew worse. When she heard about Jesus, she came up behind him in the crowd and touched his cloak, because she thought, "If I just touch his clothes, I will be healed." Immediately her bleeding stopped and she felt in her body that she was freed from her suffering.

At once Jesus realized that power had gone out from him. He turned around in the crowd and asked, "Who touched my clothes?"

"You see the people crowding against you," his disciples answered, "and yet you can ask, 'Who touched me?'" But Jesus kept looking around to see who had done it. Then the woman, knowing what had happened to her, came and fell at *his feet and, trembling with fear, told him the whole truth. He said to her, "Daughter, your faith has healed you. Go in peace and be freed from your suffering."* —Mark 5:24-34

During my struggle with health and marriage issues, the Lord kept sending me to the scripture about the woman with the issue of blood. I could relate to her because I had issues that had grown worse over the years. My issues grew until they dominated my life. There was no way to live around them because they affected my entire life. I had prayed and talked to my mother, pastor, and friends. I sought help from doctors. As I realized the Lord was ministering to me through this passage, I was relieved because I knew the ending—*she was healed.* As the years went by, I gained strength each time I heard a message taught from that passage.

The passage provides divine direction for discovering our healing:

- **Have a true desire to be healed and whole;**
- **Be willing to do your part to become healed;**
- **Identify whether healing should be physical, emotional, and/or spiritual;**
- **And be willing to do whatever it takes to become well!**

Like the woman with the issue of blood, we must believe in the healing power of Jesus. This woman had pushed her way through the crowd because she had been struggling with her condition for twelve years. The scripture states that despite her consulting many doctors, her condition grew worse. She may have heard about Jesus from the townspeople or maybe she noticed the "great multitude" gathering around Him and decided to find out what was going on. Somehow she concluded that her healing would come through Jesus. She pressed her way through the crowd. She had made up her mind, then she took action based on her belief. Something made her believe; was it her desperation? She told herself that if she just touched His garment, she would be healed. And as the healing power streamed from Jesus into her, He distinctively knew that His power had been passed to someone in the crowd. He asked the disciples specifically who touched Him. They responded, probably with frustration, "You see the people crowding against you . . . and yet you can ask, 'Who touched me?' " When the woman confessed that it was she who had received His healing power, He affirmed her by saying, _"Daughter, your faith has healed you. Go in peace and be freed from your suffering."_

That is what we must do as we deal with our issues. Whether we are dealing with health, relationship, job, children, or daily issues, we must first set our minds on the results we desire and then take action based on what we believe. We must believe that Jesus is our healer—physically, emotionally, and spiritually. If we give our issues to Him, we can become healed, delivered, and restored.

This woman had dealt with her health problem, a life-threatening condition, in many different ways. She had visited doctors, probably applied old wives' remedies, and tried solutions her friends had shared. Her family no doubt had tried to assist her, all to no avail. Blood, our life source, had been passing from her for years. If she could not identify her healing source, she would die. Do you know what it's like to have a condition or a problem you can't overcome? Have you ever tried to resolve a physical, emotional, spiritual, or relationship problem that just seemed to increase as the days turn into months and the months turn into years? Have you become numb from the frustration of trying everything only to find yourself stuck with a condition that just won't go away?

Rest assured; Jesus heals. He controls and He can deliver us from our issues. Thank God He didn't stop with that woman. He has the power to heal us today!

In the early '90s I began to have health problems. It was unusual because I had always been a very healthy person. The problems began with headaches and digestive disorders, later evolving into various stress-related conditions including gynecological disorders and ultimately ulcers. Even though I knew these were not normal, I never stopped to notice the pattern of increasing health problems nor did I stop to seek a permanent solution. I was too busy taking care of my family, my company, and my daily responsibilities.

It was not until four years later when I collapsed in my new home that I recognized that the issues had to be dealt with. You see, there is something about waking up in ICU with tubes in every crevice, hooked up to monitors, and totally immobilized that makes you face your condition. I couldn't understand why the doctors had placed me in a room with all these almost dead people!

I had issues to deal with. There was no way to continue to work around them. I needed healing physically, emotionally, and spiritually. No one could do it for me. Only Jesus could bring healing to my body, mind, and soul, but I had to do my part.

Like Jairus, I was a leader, president of my own firm. People came to me to seek help in finding their jobs and direction for their lives. I was a support system for my family, employees, and clients. When I went home at night, I had another job, taking care of my family. In the midst of meeting others' needs, I lost myself. The strain manifested itself through my health and in my marriage. I was giving but not receiving what I needed in return. Even though I expected my spouse to be supportive, I eventually realized that he could not give me what I needed. Our relationship ended in a tug of war over the business. I chose the children as my priority and sold him the business. I realized that it was more important for me to walk away from being drained emotionally, physically, and spiritually. The time had come to be healed, renewed, and restored. I had reached my point of desperation like Jairus and the woman with the issue. I needed the Lord's intervention in my life; I had to ***believe***.

II

The
Journey

CHAPTER 5

*Recognizing
the Real Enemy—
Spiritual Warfare*

O ne of the keys to handling our issues is recognizing our struggles in the spiritual realm. As we see what happens around us with physical eyes, we must understand what is actually occurring spiritually. One of the reasons we, as Christians, find ourselves dealing with issues over a long period of time is that we are in spiritual warfare. Spiritual warfare is similar to normal warfare because it is a long-term, strategic battle.

Our enemy, the devil, uses simple yet sophisticated strategies to weaken and defeat us. *The enemy plants seeds of trouble with those we love, work with, and/or respect the most.* The enemy identifies those situations in our lives that are most important to us, and then he simply begins to work within those situations through people. He has studied us and knows our strengths and our weaknesses. He knew the most important thing to me in life was my family. As we look at what is happening to us, we tend to focus on individuals, not on unseen influences on those individuals. When Jesus was discussing with the disciples God's plan for Him to leave the earth, Peter said that Jesus could not leave. Jesus responded very harshly saying, "Get behind me, Satan," because he recognized Satan as the source of influence for Peter.

The enemy campaigns for our minds and our souls by distracting and destroying us in every way that he can. Do not underestimate the effectiveness of this strategy—this may be the very reason you have issues with certain people. Think about it—is it the person, the situation, or the condition that you are succumbing to? To whom or what are you directing your anger? If we focus our anger against people, not the unseen forces, we are allowing the enemy to have the victory!

One of the ways we can tell the difference between a problem and an issue is that a problem is short-term (months) and an issue is long-term (years). *Spiritual warfare* lasts over long periods of time; it includes problems and issues. Remember, when you are in a fight, you must recognize the enemy before you can defend yourself effectively. The Word says that we fight not with people, but with principalities—that is referring to the spiritual realm of our struggle.

Finally, be strong in the Lord and in his mighty power. Put on the full armor of God so that you can take your stand against the devil's schemes. For our struggle is not against flesh and blood, but against the rulers, against the authorities, against the powers of this dark world and against the spiritual forces of evil in the heavenly realms. —Ephesians 6:10-12

The good news is that if we were not on the battlefield for the Lord, the enemy would not come after us in such an aggressive manner. We know that victory is ours because our Lord has already defeated the enemy. Whatever happens to us can only occur through the Lord's permissive will; He has to allow it to happen.

Again we must recognize how the enemy attempts to deceive us so that we don't recognize whom we are dealing with—HIM! If we think that our battle is against that job, husband, child, relative, friend, person, or situation, we need to analyze whether the enemy is using it to bring about conflict and strife. The situation or person is not always the problem; sometimes it is Satan! Spiritual warfare looks like something or someone is wreaking havoc in our lives. The enemy has used both my health and my marriage to wage warfare against me. He knows that if he can successfully attack the family, he has a good chance of winning the war because his next strategy is to attack our children. As we fight this warfare, we become increasingly frustrated, angry, disillusioned, and hopeless, yet the Lord has given us the ultimate weapon—His Word!

A word of caution: Before you decide that you are in spiritual warfare, be sure that you are not the source of your problems. Pray and ask God to reveal whether your issues are spiritual, physical, or emotional issues. Ask Him if you need to bring more order and discipline into your life or if you are in warfare. For example, there are people who are in a constant struggle. They are always late for appointments, their family is always in crisis, they never finish projects they start, they lose their jobs, or they are constantly running to the utilities office just before the electricity is cut off.

These situations can occur because we lack the ability to prioritize what is important in our life. Instead of planning and prioritizing time, finances, and other resources, we allow life to manage us. But when we live our lives according to the priorities outlined in the Word, our lives will be manageable. If you have done all that you can according to the Word and like the woman with the issue of blood have exhausted every resource to solve your problem—and the crisis prevails—you are probably in spiritual warfare.

> *The Lord is my light and my salvation—*
> > *whom shall I fear?*
> *The Lord is the stronghold of my life—*
> > *of whom shall I be afraid?*
> *When evil men advance against me*
> > *to devour my flesh,*
> *when my enemies and my foes attack me,*
> > *they will stumble and fall.*
> *Though an army besiege me,*
> > *my heart will not fear;*
> *though war break out against me,*
> > *even then will I be confident.*
>
> *One thing I ask of the Lord,*
> > *this is what I seek:*
> *that I may dwell in the house of the Lord*

all the days of my life,
to gaze upon the beauty of the Lord
and to seek him in his temple.
For in the day of trouble
he will keep me safe in his dwelling;
he will hide me in the shelter of his tabernacle
and set me high upon a rock.
Then my head will be exalted
above the enemies who surround me;
at his tabernacle will I sacrifice with shouts of joy;
I will sing and make music to the Lord.

—Psalm 27: 1-6

CHAPTER 6

A Strategic Weapon: Mental Abuse

"You can't do anything right. . . ."

"You don't deserve. . . ."

"You can't be successful."

"You aren't anything and you'll never be anything."

"You can't make it in the world on your own."

"You aren't good enough. . . ."

"You don't have enough sense to. . . ."

Pain, excruciating, unending pain, the worst kind of pain, yet it is not physical. Consistent patterns of excessiveness. Extreme highs and lows. Cold distant behavior and sexual denial for months on end. Mental or emotional abuse is an effective way of controlling and manipulating someone else's behavior. Unlike physical abuse, it is hard to see, yet it leaves mental, emotional, and invisible scars. It is the abuse that society has not dealt with or very few people discuss. When the word "abuse" comes to mind, the first reaction is to consider physical abuse or substance abuse. We hear and see daily bouts of physical abuse, but when was the last time you heard or read about people who are mentally abused?

When I read *I, TINA* in the early '90s, it was amazing how much I related to this superstar who had survived a toxic relationship. The epilogue read, "What was it like when I walked out and left Ike? Yeah—I was afraid. But sometimes you've got to let everything go—purge yourself. I did that. I

had nothing, but I had my freedom. My message here, and
I do hope that in this book there is a message for people, is:
If you are unhappy with anything—your mother, your father,
your husband, your wife, your job, your boss, your car—whatever is bringing you down, get rid of it. Because you'll find
that when you're free, your true creativity, your true self comes
out."

I identified with Tina, not from physical abuse, but mental
abuse . . . that illusive abuse that can linger without your
even being conscious of what you're experiencing until it has
its compounded effect on you. I do not endorse divorce,
but when you are involved in a relationship that tears you
down mentally, emotionally, physically, or spiritually, you must
analyze whether you should stay in the relationship. Choose
the type of intervention to employ based upon the amount
of damage to your life and the willingness of your partner
to seek help. Intervention may be in the form of counseling,
separation from the abuser, or both depending on the extent
of the abuse. It is best to seek outside intervention in any
case of abuse.

From a spiritual perspective, mental abuse originates from
the enemy; it is an effective weapon of spiritual warfare. The
abuser allows the enemy to use him or her to control and
ultimately destroy you. Demonic forces can dominate our life
if we allow them to. Mental abuse is a strategic attack by the
enemy; if he can destroy your mental health, self-confidence,

and esteem, you will be destroyed. Anyone who mentally abuses another is focused on controlling his victim. The abuser does not use physical abuse since there is public evidence of that type of abuse.

Mental abuse is a strategic attack on the mind. The goal of the abuser is to control and manipulate. Mental abuse can be administered in subtle ways; it is spoken, and sometimes communicated in a nonverbal way. It can be very difficult to detect. It is a strategic weapon because the abused does not always realize she is being abused. Mental abuse occurs through the constant conditioning of the mind in ways which negatively impact the abused. The abuser plants thoughts into the mind that ultimately cause the abused to consider herself ineffective. The goal of the abuser is to control and manipulate by making the abused think that there is something wrong with her.

Mental abuse is a powerful weapon because it is a negative conditioning of the mind against yourself. Those who use mental abuse are cunning because they know that the abused can be manipulated to appear mentally unstable. This form of abuse leaves no physical evidence; there are no visible scars. It is powerful and effective because it causes extensive damage. A friend of mine heard it described like this, "Mental abuse is the deliberate and systematic diminishing of another person's mind and esteem."

The mental abuser uses phrases like "You don't deserve...,"

"You're losing your mind. . . ," "You cannot. . . . ," "You are not designed to. . . ." In other words he concentrates on tearing you down. From experience I can tell you that even those of us who have strong minds can be controlled by mental abuse because it stifles the way we feel about ourselves. Mental abuse also occurs through mind games which are designed to manipulate the victim. These games are usually played to evoke reactions to various situations and environments. For example, a husband may withhold affection from his wife to punish her. If you need to evaluate whether you are involved in an abusive situation, watch the person's actions and listen to what is being said to you. If the messages you are receiving are consistently negative, you are probably in an abusive relationship.

It is ironic that the mental abuser may or may not be intellectually strong but usually has serious street smarts. He knows that planting certain thoughts into his victim's mind will evoke predictable reactions. This type of abuser knows how to push all the right buttons, how to manipulate, and how to create perceptions. The abuser's intention is to break you mentally because if he can destroy your mind, you cannot survive. The mental abuser may plant thoughts which make you believe that you are losing your mind or about to have a nervous breakdown. He can take a positive situation and put a negative spin on it or he may turn simple situations into chaos to create a perception of your mental instability, not only to you but also to others.

This brings me to another very important point: **Recognize people for who they are, not for who you want them to be.** We sometimes underestimate how serious the enemy is about destroying us and how he uses people who are close to us to do just that. When you see anyone doing things to undermine you physically, mentally, or emotionally, don't just stand there; get away from him! Yes, as Christians we should pray for our enemies, but if they are seeking to destroy us, we must exercise self-preservation, which usually means putting distance between us and them.

Beware, mental abuse can be so subtle that you may not see or feel it until the cumulative effect occurs. It can be administered in small daily doses. Listen to what is being said to you—is it building you up or tearing you down? Are the messages you hear making you question yourself? Is your mind subconsciously processing negative thoughts about you because of what you are hearing? Are you allowing others to define who you are or complete you?

Anyone who mentally abuses other people is extremely dangerous. The abuser's desperation causes the desire to control and manipulate. The desperate person will lie, cheat, and do whatever it takes to control people around him. And because he doesn't want to be perceived negatively, he will sometimes take on a Jekyll/Hyde personality. His public personality may be charming, courteous, and engaging while he is hostile, self-centered, and arrogant within his private environment. **If you are involved in a mentally abusive relationship, get help!** If not, it will destroy you. Mental abuse can be as dangerous as physical abuse. It is dangerous because it can be totally invisible, yet completely erosive to your mental health.

If anyone is repeatedly telling you who you are not, what you cannot do, and what you can't be, he is doing it to destroy who you are. The person and the enemy know if they can condition your mind against who you are, you will be destroyed. Don't even engage in light conversation with that person because he will pepper his conversation with negative comments and mind games to confuse you. He understands that if he can undermine your thoughts, he can control your life.

The situation can be complex because the abuser may have convinced himself and others that he loves you and whatever he is doing is for your "best interest." Ask the Lord for guidance and analyze whether the actions you question are consistent with the Word. As Christian couples, it is our responsibility to live under the authority of God, and it is the male's responsibility to lead his family under God's leadership. If our spouse makes decisions and operates from his or her own agenda, *our best interest is not the goal.*

As a victim of mental abuse, I can attest to its debilitating effects. Because the nature of the abuse is cumulative, so is the reversal process. If you have been mentally abused, you cannot expect the effect to go away as soon as the abuse ends. It takes long-term focused effort for recovery. It may take as long to recover from the abuse as the amount of time you endured and recognized the abuse. Your restoration is a process—it takes prayer, faith, time, constant affirmation, and sometimes counseling to diagnose and treat this form of abuse effectively.

How do you know when it's time to end the abusive relationship? When you know that the abuser does not have the capacity nor the willingness to change. Do not make a decision based on emotion or one single action. Watch for a pattern of behavior to determine what you need to do to protect yourself. Look at the whole picture, not just bits and pieces. We must put our experiences in perspective to determine our course of action. Evaluate whether your partner has integrity. Watch how he treats family and friends. How does he select his friends? Is he responsible, respectful, and reliable? Is he willing to be accountable for his actions?

Mental abuse was a strategic weapon in my spiritual warfare. It was hidden in the pursuit of the good life—a family, a relationship, and a business. It was not until things went very wrong that I stopped to see it for what it was, a battle for my life.

CHAPTER 7

Codependence — An Attack by the Enemy

hen you see the word "codependence,"
what do you think?
Codependence may not mean anything to you,
or you may be familiar with the clinical term. It is difficult
to explain the condition in a sentence or even a paragraph.
Codependence is a relationship involving a person who has an
addictive or compulsive disorder and his partner, who takes
on the responsibilities of the relationship. It occurs when one
partner assumes a caretaking disposition for the other and
loses herself while taking on the burdens of the troubled partner. In the process, the supportive partner loses her self-esteem
and self-worth as she builds her world around the troubled
partner. The codependent relationship happens whether the
addictive/compulsive partner has acknowledged his condition
or not. Codependency occurs because someone in the relationship has to be responsible.

My first recognition of being in a codependent relationship
was after fifteen years of marriage. I had watched as early
business success for my husband had changed from one dilem-
ma to another. Through the years he was involved in a number
of business deals, all of which eventually failed for various
reasons. The failures had a tremendous impact on our marriage; there was no financial stability and our relationship was
strained. Each time a venture failed, my husband's ego was
deflated and my role was to be his cheerleader.

If I, the enabler, tried to hold him, the codependent, accountable for the risk that he took repeatedly by putting our family's financial stability in jeopardy, my commitment to "for better or for worse" was questioned. I was accused of being supportive during the successful times and ready to give up when things got tough. What I did not realize until the marriage was almost over was that he had demons to face from the past. He could not be happy with me because he was not happy with himself.

We came from different worlds, I from a Christian family, the youngest of six children and very sheltered. His was a stormy childhood filled with episodes of anger, violence, and daily doses of street life. There were family secrets, yet in spite of the bondage in his life, he was socially acceptable because of the economic status of his family. I did not recognize the patterns of excessiveness that came to dominate our lives—the desire to succeed at any cost, unresolved anger, lack of communication, and the mental abuse. Our family was in warfare. The bondage of his childhood was alive and destroying our relationship. Unresolved issues that had nothing to do with me kept haunting him and growing as he tried to pretend that they did not exist. He blamed me for problems he was not willing to address about himself. No amount of success, financial or material, was enough to keep our family together.

A scripture which speaks to codependence is Galatians 6:4, 5, *"Each one should test his own actions. Then he can take pride*

in himself, without comparing himself to somebody else, for each
one should carry his own load." As a wife, I understood that
my role was to support my husband, and I did even though
I recognized that he was not learning lessons with each new
venture. Later I discovered that there were secrets and lies in
spite of the fact that I continued to be there for him.

Author Melody Beattie discusses codependence in
Codependent No More. She writes, "A codependent person is
one who has let another person's behavior affect him or her,
and who is obsessed with controlling that person's behavior."
She further states that, "The other person might be a child, an
adult, a lover, a spouse, a brother, a sister, a grandparent, a
client, or a best friend. He or she could be an alcoholic, a drug
addict, a mentally or physically ill person, a normal person who
occasionally has sad feelings, . . . but *the heart of the definition*
and recovery lies not in the other person—no matter how much
we believe it does. It lies in ourselves, in the ways we have
let other people's behavior affect us and in the ways we try to
affect them: the obsessing, the controlling, the obsessive "helping," caretaking, low self-worth bordering on self-hatred, self-
repression, abundance of anger and guilt, peculiar dependency
on peculiar people, attraction to and tolerance for the bizarre,
other-centeredness that results in abandonment of self, communication problems, intimacy problems, and an ongoing whirl-
wind trip through the five-stage grief process [*emphasis added*].

Beattie further explains that "one fairly common denominator was having a relationship, personally or professionally, with troubled, needy, or dependent people. But a second, more common denominator seemed to be the unwritten, silent rules that usually develop in the immediate and set the pace for relationships. The rules prohibit discussion about problems; open expression of feelings; direct, honest communication; realistic expectations, such as being human, vulnerable, or imperfect; selfishness; trust in other people and one's self; playing and having fun; and rocking the delicately balanced family canoe through growth and change—however healthy and beneficial that movement might be. These rules are common to alcoholic family systems but can emerge in other families too."

A SOURCE OF CODEPENDENT BEHAVIOR

As I researched codependence, I discovered that one must always look at family backgrounds; psychologists refer to "the family of origin." Though each of our families has its own peculiarities, we must learn to recognize normal versus abnormal behavior. Most families have varying degrees of dysfunctional behavior; however, when the abnormal dominates the normal, the impact affects the current and future family. This cycle continues until members recognize, then actively work to break the cycle. *LIFE Support Leader's Handbook*, compiled by Johnny Jones, characterizes a dysfunctional family:

- A dysfunctional family focuses its attention on an emotionally needy family member.
- A dysfunctional family places limits on the expression of feelings.
- A dysfunctional family discourages open talk about obvious problems.
- A dysfunctional family permits destructive roles for the children in the family.
- A dysfunctional family fails to provide appropriate nurture for developing children.
- A dysfunctional family is closed to the outside world.

As a result of living within a dysfunctional family, my self-esteem was totally gone. I lost myself and my perspective of what is "normal." It became more and more difficult to maintain my identity. I lost the ability to get in touch with my feelings; I denied and repressed them. The ulcers developed and I experienced chronic depression. This became a way of life. I found validation through and was very good at taking care of others while neglecting myself and my feelings.

In Pastor West's sermon, "Do You Want to Be Made Well?" he defined codependence as "dependence upon other people for our emotional stability." West commented that "codependents are always looking to someone for the approval of someone else." The irony of codependency, as West eloquently explained, is that "once we've grown dependent upon others to care for ourselves, then we find that 'I don't have anyone to take care of me!'"

THE SOLUTION

The solution is simple, yet complex—it's self-care! Yes, do the unthinkable—**take care of yourself first.** Open your heart to you; listen to what your heart says you want and need. Trust yourself. Do not depend on others as a source for your happiness. Start meeting your own needs and fulfilling your desires. If you've been in a codependent behavior pattern, breaking out will take some time and significant changes. You've probably been making sure someone, if not everyone, is taken care of, except yourself. Start by thinking about what you want. If you're like me, it had been so long since I thought like that, I literally did not know what I wanted. But stick with it. When you're asked a question as simple as what you would like to eat, decide—don't say "I don't know" or "I don't care" or "You decide." Start making decisions about what works for you. And don't be surprised when your codependent partner thinks you've lost your mind or tries to convince you that you have. He is not accustomed to your thinking of yourself and it will probably seem a bit bizarre that you aren't focusing on his needs as you have in the past.

One of the keys to recovering from codependence is what

Melody Beattie refers to as "learning the art of acceptance," which means to accept people and situations as they are, not trying to control the outcome, but learning to take life as it comes. In other words, stop resisting. A friend of mine calls it, "Let go and let God." It sounds so much simpler than it really is—for me.

I'm the person who has to read the Serenity Prayer daily, and on some days hourly. It reads:

> God, grant me the serenity
> To accept the things I cannot change,
> Courage to change the things I can,
> And wisdom to know the difference.

The Word also affirms our identity in Christ: *"But you are a chosen people, a royal priesthood, a holy nation, a people belonging to God, that you may declare the praises of him who called you out of darkness into his wonderful light"* —1 Peter 2:9.

I now understand why the Lord kept sending me this scripture while I was going through my separation and divorce: *"Trust in the Lord with all your heart and lean not on your own understanding; in all your ways acknowledge him, and he will make your paths straight"* —Proverbs 3:5-6. Another translation reads, "He will direct thy paths." I needed direction and I needed to trust Him who was truly worthy of my trust. Somehow I started to put my total trust into someone who could not help me any more than I could help myself. I was lost; I did not understand how my life could have become so unmanageable. I needed to trust and believe in the Lord who was and is the true navigator of my life. I had to put my life back into His hands.

Codependence was one of my issues; it is also a part of my journey to faith, healing, renewal, and restoration. I hope that by acknowledging this issue, it will somehow assist you in recognizing yours and ultimately starting your own journey to wholeness!

CHAPTER 8

*Gearing Up
for the Battle*

*A*s you look at your life, you may recognize
there were certain points that prepared
your battles. You were in boot camp trai
Boot camp is that period of life that breaks you dow
which your freedom is taken away. It occurs when yo
stripped of your privileges and you have to earn ever
most basic privileges back by totally submitting to au
In boot camp your environment is totally structured.
no decisions to make—you are told when to eat, how
when to bathe, and what to use when you bathe. Boo
designed to break you systematically to a point where
easily submit and do as you are told. It prepares you
adversity and teaches survival skills for warfare.

The result of successfully completing boot camp is t
as you have been broken piece by piece, you are resto
by piece without realizing it. It is conditioning of the
body. Upon completion, your body is in mint conditi
self-esteem is high, and you take pride in your accom
ments. You are ready for warfare!

Most of life's lessons which I learned prior to marr
shaped by my father and mother. My father taught m
independent, work hard, and not to have such a bad
My mother taught me to love myself, take care of my
and that "all that glitters ain't gold." As I talk to oth
about their lives, I realize how blessed my life has bee

family lived the abundant life. We had plenty of everything we needed—food, a home, and a truly loving family. Both parents tried to equip me for the battles of life—with the armor of God.

> *Therefore put on the full armor of God, so that when the day of evil comes, you may be able to stand your ground, and after you have done everything, to stand. Stand firm then, with the belt of truth buckled around your waist, with the breastplate of righteousness in place, and with your feet fitted with the readiness that comes from the gospel of peace. In addition to all this, take up the shield of faith, with which you can extinguish all the flaming arrows of the evil one. Take the helmet of salvation and the sword of the Spirit, which is the word of God. And pray in the Spirit on all occasions with all kinds of prayers and requests. With this in mind, be alert and always keep on praying for all the saints.* — Ephesians 6:13-18

Having a firm foundation helped me survive my boot camp experiences. When it comes to spiritual warfare, the Word teaches us to use:

- **The Belt of Truth**
- **The Breastplate of Righteousness**
- **Feet Fitted with the Gospel of Peace**

- **The Shield of Faith**
- **The Helmet of Salvation**
- **The Sword of the Spirit which is the Word of God**
- **Prayer**

The Belt of Truth—The truth is the Spirit. The Holy Spirit leads, guides, and protects us. It is that inner voice that tells us what to do. If we are Spirit-led, we can prepare and plan for our battles through its guidance. The belt holds our armor and weapons in place, just as our belts hold our clothes in place. If an item hangs from the belt, the enemy may grab it and use it against us. The belt allows us to keep our hands free for battle.

The Breastplate of Righteousness—The breastplate protects the heart of righteousness, goodness, and holiness within us. The breastplate protects our heart, the center of who we are. This covering is the reinforcement which assures protection of the heart, which also controls the mind. Your heart determines who you are and what you do. This second line of defense is there to protect us in case something harmful gets past the shield.

Feet Fitted with the Gospel of Peace—Our feet provide mobility and stability. They give us an option to stand, to fight, or to flee. They are also a point of weakness because if they are not properly covered, the feet or ankles can

...roken, leaving us totally immobilized. The gospel of
the peace of God which is beyond understanding. It
...rene confidence that He is in control and will fight
...es if we just stand.

...**Shield of Faith**—The shield is designed to protect
...he weapon that repels the fiery darts shot at us.
...use the shield of faith properly, we deflect the attack
...emy by being obedient to God even before we see
...nce of winning the battle. Faith is the "substance of
...ped for"; it is the blind confidence that we place in
...t He will protect us and enable us to win life's battles.
...he opposite of faith. We have been commanded to live
...r but in the mighty power of God.

...**Helmet of Salvation**—The helmet protects the
...control center of our being. The brain is the engine
...ly; it must be completely protected at all times. The
...he center for processing the information from other
...e body. Our salvation is our guarantee that we are
...grace. Salvation protects the soul and spirit as a
...otects the head.

...**word of the Spirit which is the Word of**
...sword is used to pierce, slice, and attack the enemy.
...upon which commands respect by all. When we
...ce, or attack the enemy, it should be with the Word
...The sword is an offensive and defensive weapon. The
...God directs, corrects, and protects us.

Prayer—Prayer is our strategic communication to
fighting spiritual warfare. As we go boldly before the
asking for His intercession and protection, it allows t
communication necessary for winning our battles. O
must hear our requests and thanksgiving, and we mu
available to hear and follow His commands for defea
enemy.

I'll share with you my strategic weapon for warfar
a prayer that I rely on for small or big challenges, an
my prayer for you:

For this reason, I kneel before the Father, from who
whole family in heaven and on earth derives its name
that out of his glorious riches he may strengthen you
through his Spirit in your inner being, so that Christ
in your hearts through faith. And I pray that you, be
and established in love, may have power, together wi
the saints, to grasp how wide and long and high and
is the love of Christ, and to know this love that surpa
knowledge—that you may be filled to the measure of
ness of God. Now to him who is able to do immeasur
than all we ask or imagine, according to his power th
work within us, to him be glory in the church and in
Jesus throughout all generations, forever and ever! An
— Ephesians 3:14-21

CHAPTER 9

Waging the Battle of the Mind

he direction for our lives starts within our minds. The introductory letter to my husband stated that I had to reorganize my mind. It meant that I had begun a process of reprogramming my mind to restore my spiritual, physical, and emotional health. I had set my mind on my desire, which was to become whole again. Since the mind is where our actions originate, I organized every aspect of my to life to become WHOLE!

I am not saying name it, claim it, and it will happen. I believe that each aspect—mind, soul, and body—must work together to bring about the change we desire, and we can receive the healing we desire *if it is within God's will.* Healing and restoration begin within our minds.

Whether we realize it or not, the mind is the headquarters for our body and our being. The mind determines how we live our lives by processing the information it receives. It shapes our perspective of the world around us. Our minds have the power to make our bodies active or inactive. Once we understand the power of our minds, we can take steps toward making what seems to be the impossible happen.

The Word says of the mind:

> *Do not conform any longer to the pattern*
> *of this world, but be transformed by the renewing*
> *of your mind. Then you will be able to test and*
> *approve what God's will is—his good, pleasing*
> *and perfect will.* —Romans 12:2

Set your minds on things above, ___
not on earthly things. — Colossians 3:2

We must be mindful of the information that we allow ourselves to listen to; it shapes the way we think. If we listen
to positive messages, our minds will be filled with positive
thoughts. If we expose ourselves to negative messages, negativ-
ity will prevail in our minds. That is why it is so important
to choose deliberately what we listen to and watch and the
environment we live and work in. They have a profound effect
on our minds and our children's minds and perspectives. We
are to some extent a product of our environment and we choose
how we live by selecting the information we allow our minds
to receive.

We often hear about the power of the tongue and the effect it
has on our lives and others. We have the power to speak things
into our lives, and we can definitely affect others by what we
say to them both positively and negatively. Do you realize that
it is the mind that controls the tongue? Could that be the
reason the Word says to "take every thought captive"?

When I started writing this book, each morning at 4:00
a.m. the Holy Spirit would awaken me to write. I had been
waking up at this time for a couple of weeks, but since I
didn't know why I woke up, I'd check on my children and go
back to bed. At our annual women's church conference, one of
the seminars was on managing our time and priorities. I was

reminded that I had slipped out of the habit of spending time with the Lord the first thing each morning; therefore my days were totally unorganized and out of control. By nature I am an early riser. Morning is when I think clearest, and it is the only time of day when I do not have distractions and interruptions. When you start your day at 4:00 a.m., you must pace yourself throughout the day to be productive continuously. As a single parent with two children, my days are very long. Our evenings are filled with dinner, activities, homework, projects, etc.

After a couple of weeks of rising at 4:00 a.m., I became very tired and spent a weekend in bed trying to recover. In spite of knowing that this book was Spirit-inspired, I also knew my body was tired. I realized that I must take control over my mind in order to complete this assignment. I made up my mind to complete it no matter what obstacles might arise. The Holy Spirit was my built-in alarm; I awoke at 4:00 a.m. daily for months. That was enough proof that this book is God's will for my life.

The next step was to program my mind and body to work in unison. Likewise, the key to our deliverance and restoration is to make up our minds that these two results can and will occur. The woman with the issue of blood had made up her mind that Jesus could heal her if she only touched the hem of His garment. Deliverance and healing are a process, and making up our minds sometimes can take months or years. We delay our blessings when we procrastinate.

I constantly wonder why it takes us so long to believe what the Lord has promised us, *"Ask and it will be given to you; seek and you will find; knock and the door will be opened to you"* —Matthew 7:7. We must ask ourselves, do we believe Jesus can heal us? Does He care or want to get involved in every detail of our lives? Or is it that we don't believe in ourselves? We are His children, born to receive our inheritance—what father doesn't want the best for his children?

When we don't trust in His promises, are we living our lives to the fullest? We are actually expressing our lack of faith in Him. Jesus said that He came "that we may have life, and have it abundantly"! So why do we choose to live a mediocre life, one that anyone can live? It starts with our minds. We must condition our minds for success, and we must be willing to pay the price. I didn't say sacrifice our children or families; we must maintain our priorities yet get the things done that need to be done.

Some of us have a tendency to be superwomen; that is not what I'm speaking of. I am addressing getting the right things done, accomplishing the will of God in our lives. **It does not mean that everything will get done, but that the important things will be handled.**

The Word says that *"as he thinketh in his heart, so is he"* Proverbs 23:7, (King James Version). We are whatever we believe about ourselves. Our reality begins to change when what we think about ourselves changes. If you know what you want from life, and if you are willing to work for what you want and trust God to do His part, chances are you will succeed. If you do not believe that you can attain your goals, you probably will not experience the life you want. You must believe in yourself.

It all starts within our minds; it is a powerful tool. If you think about it, many things around us began in the mind. Someone had to think it before it came into existence—our homes, transportation, jobs, schools, clothes, all began in someone's mind as a concept. The concept had to be developed and communicated to others and ultimately constructed into reality. That is what must happen with our healing, deliverance, and restoration—we must conceptualize, believe, make up our mind, and act on faith. Waging and winning the battle of the mind are mandatory for our healing!

RENEWING THE MIND

The Word tells us to *"be transformed by the renewing of your mind"* —Romans 12:2. In order to renew your mind, you must begin to feed it with that which will renew it. It is a conscious conditioning process whereby you feed the mind things that will strengthen it. Just as you recondition your body—focusing on what goes into your body—realize that conditioning also strengthens the mind. Feed your mind with the Word through

Christian reading, music, meditation, radio, tapes, etc. Keep feeding your mind with that which will help your mind become reconditioned. Help your mind to breathe by exposing it to new information. The mind is your body's computer. As it receives information, it stores it to be retrieved as needed. The Word should be processed and internalized to become the living word alive in you!

Just as the body needs discipline for renewal and restoration, so does the mind. Start a routine: if you rise early, start your day by reading and meditating on the promises of God. Spend time in prayer and thanksgiving, and always allow time to hear from the Lord. If you are not an early riser, schedule your prayer time during the time of the day when you have the fewest distractions. You will find that your days are more productive and you become encouraged more each day. It's similar to a physical workout; you must plan and pursue it in a disciplined manner in order to get the maximum benefit. If you can practice anything for twenty-one consecutive days, it will become a part of your life. I have written a journal for you to use as a tool for renewing your mind. Please use *The Journal of My Journey* to begin your renewal process and to document your journey.

Once you commit to your renewal, the enemy will place obstacles in front of you to discourage you. Do not fear! It only means that the Lord has deliverance for you on the other side! Recognize those inconveniences as schemes of the enemy, then press your way through the obstacles. Remember the Lord is on your side "No weapon that is formed against you shall prosper" Isaiah 54:17, (The Ryrie Study Bible).

CHAPTER 10

Talking Yourself through the Battles of Life

*D*uring a women's conference, Dr. Carolyn
Knight, assistant professor of homiletics at
the Interdenominational Theological Center in
Atlanta, Georgia, preached a message entitled "When You
Talk to Yourself," based on Mark 5. Until I heard her sermon, I had no idea how much what we say to ourselves
influences us. For years I had heard the clichés about our
being what we think and say we are. I knew intellectually that
I had the power to think my way into or out of most situations,
yet when she said, "When you talk to yourself positively, you
begin the healing process within," I truly began to understand
the importance of what I say to myself!

You see, I am one who talks to myself and lately I had been
saying very negative things to me about me. I had been telling
myself things that tore me down, not empowering messages.
It really didn't matter what others said because I was doing
an excellent job of telling myself what I could not do, why
I wasn't happy, and making excuses for not doing what I
could do. We are sometimes our worst enemy because we help
others tear us down by thinking and speaking negatively about
ourselves.

I realized in 1994 that I was going to write books. I
recognized that the Lord had given me a talent of writing. I
have a degree in journalism. I kept asking Him to use me,
but I did not want nor expect this book to be His response.
He had given me a story, a testimony. I had experienced the

peaks and valleys of a roller coaster relationship and business ventures during the last several years. Some of my closest friends knew about my health issues, but I certainly wasn't telling anyone the whole story. Some of my employees had witnessed incidents relating to the business and my husband. I'm a private person, so whatever anyone knew was only bits and pieces. My own mother didn't know much of what I had gone through until it was over. It is amazing how the mind works; I realize now that mine has blocked out many of the unpleasant incidents that occurred. Often as my daughter and I talk, she reminds me of other incidents that I have forgotten.

In order for us to rise above the challenges of life, we must empower ourselves by saying positive and affirming words. We must focus on the positive aspects of our lives, tell ourselves that we are God's child and therefore we have a guaranteed inheritance. We are descendants of royalty. *We must condition our minds for healing, restoration, and success.* When we hear negative comments about us, that is the enemy at war to destroy us. We cannot let him win the battle by allowing him to speak negative thoughts into our minds. Nor can we speak negatively about ourselves. Every time you begin to talk about yourself, say positive, affirming phrases such as "I can," "I will," "I am." As Dr. Knight reminded us, we must be like *The Little Engine That Could* who said, "I think I can, I think I can, I think I can!" Dr. Knight referred us to Mark 5 where *the woman* with the issue of blood *said to herself,* "If I just

touch his garment, I will be healed." The key is that she *said
it to herself.* What we say to ourselves opens us to God's
blessings or shuts us down.

Talking ourselves through the battles of life is the reason
the Word says, "As he thinketh in his heart, so is he." If
we think good things about ourselves, we can recognize the
goodness within us. If we pray with confidence, believe and
affirm ourselves, we can be healed.

If you don't talk to yourself, begin by saying good things to
you about you. When you talk to your children, family, and
friends, say affirming and positive words. You will find that
they enjoy being in your presence because you are blessing
them. When you are in the company of your enemy, say
positive, complimentary, encouraging, and supportive
statements—it is one of the simplest ways we can be a
light in today's world.

When you need reassurance of who you are and what you
deserve, God's Word will remind you of His promises and
who He says you are. Remember Philippians 4:13: *"I can do
everything through him (Christ) who gives me strength."*

As people in high demand, we are bombarded with
information daily. We talk to mates, children, friends, family,
coworkers, clients, vendors, doctors, clerks, even strangers. This
is the age of high-volume communication. We receive messages
daily via our computers, PDAs, cell phones, telephones, televi-
sions, radios, newspapers, and fax machines. With so many

messages bombarding us, it can sometimes become difficult to discern where and who our thoughts are coming from. We must develop and maintain a close relationship with the Holy Spirit, who leads, guides, and instructs us. When there is confusion about our thoughts, the Holy Spirit can assist us by sifting our thoughts, allowing us to realize the source of our thought life. If we do not allow the Holy Spirit to help us discern whether our thoughts are of the Lord or from the enemy, we could become confused and act based on miscommunication. We must be on alert to internalize that which delivers, not destroys, us.

Talking to ourselves and allowing the Holy Spirit to screen our messages is one of the best strategies for becoming whole again. Learn to think and speak positive truth into your life today.

III

Restoration

CHAPTER 11

Steps to Restoration

A large crowd followed and pressed around him. [25]And a woman was there who had been subject to bleeding for twelve years. [26]She had suffered a great deal under the care of many doctors and had spent all she had, yet instead of getting better she grew worse. [27]When she heard about Jesus, she came up behind him in the crowd and touched his cloak, [28]because she thought, "If I just touch his clothes, I will be healed." [29]Immediately her bleeding stopped and she felt in her body that she was freed from her suffering.

[30]At once Jesus realized that power had gone out from him. He turned around in the crowd and asked "Who touched my clothes?"

[31]"You see the people crowding against you," his disciples answered, "and yet you can ask, 'Who touched me?'"

[32]But Jesus kept looking around to see who had done it. [33]Then the woman, knowing what had happened to her, came and fell at his feet and, trembling with fear, told him the whole truth. [34]He said to her, "Daughter, your faith has healed you. Go in peace and be freed from your suffering."
— Mark 5: 24-34

SEVEN STEPS TO RESTORATION

1. Decide to do whatever it takes to bring forth healing. (vs. 28)

2. Seek Jesus. (vs. 27)

3. Turn your issues over to Him. (vs. 27)

4. Have faith that He will heal you; then think, speak, and decide that your healing is taking place. (vs. 28)

5. Feel the evidence. (vs. 29)

6. Confess and accept your healing. (vs. 33)

7. Go in peace; move forward in your life in acceptance of your healing. (vs. 34)

CHAPTER 12

Time for an
Examination

_T_he woman with the issue of blood struggled with her condition until she realized her true healing would come only from Jesus. Her focus shifted from the remedies she had tried to receiving the healing power of Jesus. After we have identified our issues and exhausted all of our resources to resolve them, then we're ready to give them to God. But can't He handle them before those problems becomes issues or before the issues become warfare—if we give them to Him?

Why choose to use our energy managing things that our Lord can handle for us? We are accustomed to taking care of our business, to making things happen, and to being independent, but dealing with life's issues can be so much easier when we give them to Jesus with the faith that He will handle them. We should maximize on the Lord's ability to handle that which we cannot handle; we can trust and depend on Him.

Like the woman with the issue of blood, we must press our way beyond daily struggles, doubt, and fear to give our issues to Jesus. That woman worked her way through the crowd as we must work our way through our issues. When we deal with issues, we must face the facts intellectually, address them physically, and then mentally commit ourselves to the healing process. Our part may include changing our lifestyle, reconditioning our mind, cleansing our heart, or renewing our spirit. If we are faithful to the healing process, our Lord will bring His work to completion by healing us emotionally and spiritually.

According to Mark 5, the woman had been to many physicians for her condition. She had exhausted all of her resources. She had a "chronic condition"; the hemorrhage had lasted twelve years. When we find that we are dealing with a condition we cannot resolve, we should examine the situation and develop an action plan for recovery.

Each time we visit a physician, he or she inquires about our family background, our vital signs are surveyed, we report our symptoms, and then we have an examination. The physician gathers information about our condition in a variety of ways to develop a diagnosis and/or analyze the cause of our condition in order to prescribe a remedy.

The dictionary's definition for examination is "the act or process of examining or being examined; careful scrutiny or inquiry; investigation; inspection." To examine is "to inspect or scrutinize with care; investigate critically."

As we consider our issues, we must be subject to inspection. Most importantly, we must conduct a self-examination —review our history, observe the patterns in our life, consider how we've taken care of ourselves, take a close look at our vital signs, and evaluate the cause of our condition. It is a process, not like those fifteen-minute visits with the family physician. Physicians are trained extensively to survey the facts and arrive at a conclusion in a matter of minutes. Or they may order additional tests to diagnose the patient's condition. As you examine yourself, take your time, gather all the information, look at family history. Not having the right information or all the information could cause the wrong diagnosis. You can't risk that; you are too precious to our Lord. You are His child; He wants only the best for you.

The key is to be painfully honest with yourself and with the Lord. He knows your condition; He is the Great Physician. You must be willing to lay yourself before Him after you have conducted your self-examination. It will not be pretty. You will see things you have looked over many, many times. You will notice patterns of behavior and symptoms. You may even realize the cause of your condition. Your conclusion will lead you to the next step in this process.

The Lord knows that until our issues have severely affected our lives, we tend not to deal with them. We continue to push them aside; they are usually not investigated until they dominate our lives. But until we are ready to examine what is really going on, we cannot be a candidate for healing and restoration. Sometimes it takes extreme situations for us to get to the point where we will stop to survey our emotions, our intellect, our spiritual and physical being. I knew that things were not in order in my life. I knew that there were issues, but it took a couple of near-death experiences to get my attention. You do not have to wait until your condition is so severe. Watch for patterns. Recognize the condition. Take it to the Great Physician for healing and restoration.

Some of us attempt to repair whatever is broken. Others

bring us things and situations to "fix." We work on relationships, people, and problems, yet who works on us when we need it? Are we going to the right source for assistance?

That woman with the issue of blood had gone to many physicians, yet her condition grew worse! Until she met Jesus, she had not found anyone with the expertise to heal her issues!

Are we seeking healing from the Divine Healer or letting "shade-tree mechanics" look beneath our hoods? Are we seeking godly advice from seasoned Christians or do we watch talk show hosts to find our answers? Consider whom you are going to for counsel. Are they knowledgeable or wise? There is a difference. What is the source of their wisdom? When we watch television to find our answers, we see and hear the world's perspective. We are being informed and can become very knowledgeable, yet the key is the quality of the information, not the quantity. The Word is the best source of counsel for healing. Getting advice from Christians who counsel based on the Word allows us to hear God's perspective. God's word is wisdom and truth; it is the truth that sets us free.

Are we going to others with the right motive? When we go to our pastors, are we going for sympathy or to learn how to apply God's Word to our life? When we go to our pastors for spiritual guidance, we must not forget that the Lord heals. Our pastors can share their wisdom and direct us to the appropriate scriptures. Some people are chosen vessels for

healing, but God is the source of all healing. We cannot
become entangled in relationships with pastors or spiritual
leaders which undermine and violate what only the Lord can
do in our lives. Understand clearly the role others can play
in your healing. They can minister, support, and pray for
you, but you and God are partners for your healing and
deliverance.

God is our refuge and strength,
  an ever-present help in trouble.
Therefore we will not fear, though the earth give way
  and the mountains fall into the heart of the sea,
  though its waters roar and foam
  and the mountains quake with their surging.

There is a river whose streams make glad the
  city of God,
the holy place where the Most High dwells.
God is within her, she will not fall;
  God will help her at break of day.
Nations are in uproar, kingdoms fall;
  he lifts his voice, the earth melts.

The Lord Almighty is with us;
　　the God of Jacob is our fortress.

Come and see the works of the Lord,
　　the desolations he has brought on the earth.
He makes wars cease to the ends of the earth;
　　he breaks the bow and shatters the spear,
　　he burns the shields with fire.
"Be still, and know that I am God;
　　I will be exalted among the nations,
　　I will be exalted in the earth."

The Lord Almighty is with us;
　　the God of Jacob is our fortress.
　　—Psalm 46

CHAPTER 13

Faith and a Positive Attitude

But Jesus kept looking around to see who had done it. Then the woman, knowing what had happened to her, came and fell at his feet and, trembling with fear, told him the whole truth. He said to her, "Daughter, your faith has healed you. Go in peace and be freed from your suffering."

While Jesus was still speaking, some men came from the house of Jairus, the synagogue ruler. "Your daughter is dead," they said. *"Why bother the teacher any more?"*

Ignoring what they said, Jesus told the synagogue ruler, "Don't be afraid; just believe." —Mark 5:32-36

Recently as my daughter and I were riding along, we were talking about how our days had been. She knew that I was struggling with the decision of stepping out on faith into business for myself again, and she also knew that I was having a very hard time dealing with my job. I started my normal recital of how I was tired and ready to leave the job. She said to me, "Mommy, you have to decide each morning that it is going to be a good day, and when you do that, you will have a good day." The premise is a simple one—yet my reminder came from the mouth of a child.

I need constant reassurance in the area of positive thinking. The particular day my daughter spoke those words of positive assurance to me I had spent at least an hour in the parking lot with a friend who kept reminding me of God's promises for my life. She reminded me of the company I founded, the lives that had been blessed, how others were earning a living from the foundation I had laid, and the fact that I wasn't taking advantage of my own gifts and blessings. It was a sobering reminder for me of how my doubt had stifled me from living up to my own potential. Everyone else saw it, yet I allowed my doubt and fear to blind me and bind me!

When I reflect on the woman with the issue of blood, I realize that she possessed a very positive attitude—she believed if she could only touch Jesus' garment, she would be healed. And when He spoke to her, He affirmed that her faith had healed her. The Word tells us, "Faith without works is dead."

> *Now faith is being sure of what we hope for*
> *and certain of what we do not see. This is what*
> *the ancients were commended for.*
>
> *By faith we understand that the universe*
> *was formed at God's command, so that is what*
> *is seen was not made out of what was visible. . . .*
>
> *And without faith it is impossible to please*
> *God, because anyone who comes to him must*
> *believe that he exists and that he rewards those*
> *who earnestly seek him.* —Hebrews 11:1-3,6

It is our faith, not our Christianity, that sets us apart from one another—the faith that empowers our positive attitude. The Word says, "as a man thinketh, so is he." It is our faith in who God is and who we are in Him that gives us the power to do what we need to do.

Faith enables us to dream and to do the unimaginable.

And we must have faith that our issues will be resolved, that
our conditions will be healed, and that we can be restored. As
each of us experiences the challenges of life, we have issues
that keep popping up. We will be tested over and over again
on those issues until we pass the test. You see, the Lord wants
to strengthen us in the areas of our weakness, and the only
way that we can become stronger is when we have opportuni-
ties to flex and exercise those weak muscles. Once we have
conquered an area of weakness, He goes on to strengthen
another area and so it goes. Many times the Lord will work on
the same areas repeatedly because once we have strengthened
those various areas, we may lose or forget other areas that have
been built up. Our spiritual, emotional, and physical being
is under continuous construction. It is faith in our Lord who
works "all things together for good" that enables us to grow in
His grace. When we finally get to a point where we can turn
our issues over to the Lord, we experience miracles!

Our faith and attitude work in conjunction with one
another. If our faith is weak, we cannot have a positive
attitude. If our faith is truly strong, we will have a positive
attitude. So when we as Christians believe that the Lord will
fulfill His promises to us, it will be reflected in our attitude
and our actions. Doubt and fear will result in a negative
attitude. _Remember faith is the opposite of fear._ If we
listen to ourselves and others talk, we can hear our level
of faith by the confidence and assurance we communicate.

The battle of spirituality starts within our minds. Our minds shape our attitude. We must have faith to live as the Lord has commanded. Most of the time we cannot see the outcome of our situation; we simply need to remember that the Lord always keeps His promises.

"*Say, therefore, to the sons of Israel, 'I am the Lord, and I will bring you out from under the burdens of the Egyptians, and I will deliver you from their bondage. I will also redeem you with an outstretched arm and with great judgments.'*" —Exodus 6:6 (The Ryrie Study Bible)

This is the promise the Lord laid on my heart in 1994. What God promises . . . He delivers!

CHAPTER 14

Good Grief!

hew! It's over! We've been delivered; we've been healed! We are ready for restoration.

Once you recognize your healing, you can take a deep breath because you know that you are ready to move on. After you calm down from the surge of adrenaline and after you've had your time of realization, you will probably experience a grieving process. If you've had to detach from a relationship, give up some things, or get out of your comfort zone, you will need to grieve over your loss. It's OK. Most good things that come to us in life require some blood, sweat, and tears. Accept it. You've made sacrifices to experience your healing. Now it's time to feel it and move on. Many times that is easier said than done.

Depending on what you've experienced to receive your healing, it is likely that you will experience the five-step grief process. You may have lost a relationship, acquaintances, old habits, or a familiar environment. If your loss was a fixture in your life, expect to mourn that loss. The grief process includes:

- shock and denial
- anger
- grief and despair
- acceptance
- resolution

Even though you may experience the steps in different orders, working through each step is necessary to complete the grief process.

Jesus told the woman with the issue of blood to "go in peace." I suspect that the woman had grieved her losses at times during her twelve-year bout with her condition. When you have a severe loss or change in your life, allow yourself to grieve that loss. Let yourself have that experience because it is a part of your deliverance.

At times we find ourselves on an emotional roller coaster. Managing our emotions without experiencing grief can be unhealthy. When I realized that my ulcer had healed, I was elated. I told my friends and shared my testimony with the church. On the other hand, when my marriage ended—even though I saw it coming—once we were separated, I had to grieve that loss. I had grieved during the last few years as I tried to remain in it, but I hadn't let it go. When my husband was out of the house and out of my life, I had to grieve that change. During the divorce I agreed to sell the business I had founded. The grief that resulted was overwhelming; I became depressed because I had put my heart and soul into that business. I thought that it was going to be the source of income for my children and I after the divorce. It is clear today that the Lord had other plans for me.

Change is inevitable in everyone's life. It occurs more in some lives than others. I accepted a long time ago that my life would be in constant evolution. What matters is how we accept and deal with change. Denying change or working against it can be very stressful. Much of the stress we experience is simply because of how we anticipate or deal with change. If we allow things to be as they are and make adjustments to accommodate change, our lives can be simpler and less stressful. It is when we insist upon going against the grain that we experience aggravation and frustration. An old saying is, "If it don't fit, don't force it." If you can relax and let whatever it is go, you'll get better faster. Trying to control situations or people will only lead to disappointment and frustration.

Changes in your life as a result of your healing can be unsettling; allow yourself to grieve the loss so that you can move into your restoration with the strength you'll need for your journey. Know that God can fill what you perceive as a loss with more than you could possibly have imagined. Grief is an emotion. Experience it and have confidence that God always seeks our best. We must learn to look at each challenge as an opportunity for God to develop us into the people He called and created us to be.

CHAPTER 15

The Cleansing Process

*T*ake a few minutes to reflect on your issues. Afterwards, try the following mental exercise: Imagine yourself standing under a waterfall in a beautiful tropical setting; the water flows over your head and spills unto your body. As you continue to stand there, the cool water continues to flow over and throughout your body. You can feel the dirt, oil, and old skin being washed away. You can feel your supple new skin as the water both purges and renews your body. Your mind is refreshed, your body is rejuvenated, and your spirit is freed. This purging is cleansing the impurities from your body, mind, and spirit. You are clean and fresh as you walk from beneath the flowing water into a gentle breeze. You are restored—ready to move on!

A critical part of the healing, renewal, and restoration process is cleansing. The cleansing process may take place before, during, or after you have been healed and restored. In order for the process to be complete, you must experience a cleansing. I am referring to a thorough "wash," not just rinsing off. It will consist of some scrubbing and exfoliating, a thorough lathering, followed by a river rinse. It is the removal of all traces of the evidence of your battle spiritually, emotionally, and physically. It is the cleansing that refreshes you and allows you to move into the next phase of your life.

Cleansing occurs when you take time out to reflect on things that have happened, get rid of the undesirable residue, and make adjustments as necessary. Whether you take time out once or daily, remove yourself from your busy schedule and analyze changes that need to occur to move your life in the direction you want to go. Take the time and space to face your issues. Identify those areas in your life where things are fine and there is no need for change. Identify areas that need change and decide how you will make those changes. Set a strategic plan for what needs to happen to create the life you desire.

Forgiveness is an important aspect of cleansing. We must be willing to forgive those who have contributed to our issues, whether they ask for forgiveness or not. It can be very difficult to forgive someone whom you know has deliberately hurt or abused you. It is critical for you to rid yourself of the anger and animosity that grow from being deceived, humiliated, frustrated, or punished, yet when we forgive, it frees us to move into the next level of life. We cannot change what has happened to us, but we can choose not to harbor it and let it fester within us. You may need to have a conversation, write a letter, or set two chairs in a room and pretend you are talking to the offender. You cannot be renewed until you've left behind the residue from the past. Forgive as often and as many people as you need to move on; your restoration cannot be complete until you've taken this step in the cleansing process.

Your cleansing may be accomplished through meditation, fasting, a physical workout regimen, a retreat, or a baptismal-like cleansing experience. No matter what form it takes, you must remove the traces of the past in a way that is visibly evident so that you can begin anew. I believe that God uses every experience to lead us into His ultimate purpose, if we allow Him to.

There were many times when I felt like Job, who was tested in every area of his life—his family, his health, his friends, and his wealth. Each area was swept away as the enemy attempted to test Job. Job never lost faith in God because he knew that he was a man of integrity and he knew who God was. Job endured in spite of his loss of everything, and God restored two times the amount that had been taken away. Job's story demonstrates what I believe—_"And we know that God causes all things to work together for good to those who love God, to those who are called according to His purpose"_ —Romans 8:28 (The Ryrie Study Bible).

Cleansing is a demonstration of removing evidence of your issues. Choose what works for you. The method may be a one-time activity or it may be on-going. For example, it may involve a fast or several fasts. The important thing is to have a means for consciously cleaning out the residue so that you can move on to the next level and receive what God has for you. The Lord can begin His new work in you only after you have been cleansed from your past.

The cleansing phase of your deliverance and restoration is absolutely necessary to experience complete healing. Many times when we seek healing from a traditional physician, she will prescribe a medication, then instruct us to take it until it is all gone in order to avoid a relapse. Our cleansing is similar because it is a part of and not apart from healing; therefore we must be totally cleansed "to avoid a relapse."

Prayer must be a part of this cleansing for its maximum effectiveness. The Word instructs us to present our requests to the Lord in prayer and supplication. Just as I am sure that you have begun to praying about your issues, understand that it is prayer that seals your cleansing. As you present your prayer throughout your cleansing, realize prayer is an integral part of the healing experience.

The method of cleansing used for your particular healing and restoration depends on the depth of your experience. As I mentioned before, it can take place in the form of fasting, a physical work-out regimen, a retreat, or a baptismal. Ask the Holy Spirit to show you which form of cleansing is appropriate. Remember that the method chosen will correlate with the depth of the issues you are addressing. Deep issues require deep cleansing. As you reflect on the depth of your issues and their effect on your life, consider the physical evidence you need in order to be cleansed.

Cleansing gives us the space in our body, mind, and spirit to receive our new blessings.

CHAPTER 16

Go in Peace!

*I*sn't it wonderful to watch the Lord's miraculous hand work in your life? You see it each day whether you recognize it or not. Let's see—He woke you up this morning, He gave you food to eat and a place to sleep. If you think back to what you've asked Him for, I'm sure that you will recognize evidence of answered prayer. It may be something you began asking for a long time ago, and you see it developing before your eyes. Or it may be something that you've recently requested. The good news is that God is able.

As our journey comes to an end, realize that we've covered a lot of territory. We need not focus on our past, though it may be easy to do. I hope that you are ready to focus on your own journey. There is no benefit in wallowing in the past; we must let those experiences be lessons for the future. Let them go!

I've watched the Lord work in my life. I've reflected on my experiences, and I realize that I couldn't have the appreciation for what He's done for me had I not *gone through!* I tried to get stuck in them, but thank God that neither my family nor friends would let me. You too must go through. And just know that you are going through, you will be healed, you will be delivered, and you will be restored!

What do healing and restoration look like? It depends on your experience. You may see evidence of healing in your face. Look into your eyes. Are they glassy or has the sparkle returned? Does your body feel vibrant and healthy or are you feeling sluggish? I knew my healing had began when I started to feel my own feelings again. I began to feel physically healthy and vibrant again. I knew I was coming around when people began commenting that my countenance had changed, I felt alive again. I began to feel restored when I could commune with God and feel Him commune with me. You will see it in your everyday life, you will feel it, and you must believe and know that you are being restored daily.

If you believe, if you have faith—start living it! Faith is the evidence of things unseen—you must live as if you are already restored. If and when you start living in the faith that you are healed, delivered, and restored, you will begin to see the evidence. Life is what we believe it to be, good or bad, happy or sad—that is the power of the mind.

If you want just enough to get by, you'll have it if you trust God for it. If you want that abundant life that the Lord has promised, you'll have it! Trust Him; He is worthy of all your trust. He is faithful and just, and you don't have to feel guilty about your past because the Word reminds us that He will forgive all our sins. Don't keep beating yourself up, making excuses why He can't work within you. He can and He will if you just let Him.

I am always amazed at just how mighty and majestic God is. As I was writing this book, I came to a point where I stopped rising early to write. I woke up, but I made every excuse not to write. I'd pray, I'd edit, I'd think through differ- ent aspects—I procrastinated! Then He captured my attention (again). I had my monthly cycle, but, instead of it ending, it continued and continued and continued. By the tenth day I said, "Lord, what are you trying to teach me?" As a Christian who believes that there are no coincidences with God, I couldn't help but see the parallel between my condition and the woman with the issue of blood. I discussed it with my friend who was helping edit the book. Her response was that perhaps the Lord wanted me to empathize with that woman. What I have realized from that experience is that nothing really changes as you live with your issues. Sometimes we expect to see a message written across the sky or we expect things to change immediately. Don't look for your life to change so vividly. There will be a subtle progressive change, but overall life simply goes on. Your friends and family keep going on with their lives; the world around you continues to be as it always was. You simply have to see, live, and make the transitions necessary to becoming healed, renewed, and restored. The woman with the issue of blood had instan- taneous healing that came from her touching the master's garment. Her healing was His will for her life. *Our healing must be His will for our life, and we must be willing to do our part to become healed.*

Our lives are in constant transition; our healing may occur

as a transition instead of being instantaneous. Accept the healing, acknowledge it, and move on in peace. You know what peace looks like for you. If you are unsure, ask the Lord to give you His peace. He will! He gives "peace that surpasses all understanding." His peace is not a cliché. It is His peace that assures you that, no matter what happens, He is in control. It is His peace that allows you to keep moving forward when your environment would dictate that you stand still. It is His peace that is the strength that you depend on when you have none of your own. It is His peace that helps you to be still and know that He is our God who always keeps His promise!

This story would not be complete without confessing my stubbornness. After experiencing a complete healing, I fell into the cycle of not taking care of myself while I was writing this book. I became ill again with ulcers. I was admitted into critical care, this time with four bleeding ulcers, and thus the lesson began again. I have learned that *taking care of myself has to be a lifestyle, not a temporary routine, to maintain my whole well-being.* The Lord has a plan for our lives. Our experiences are our lessons; we can choose whether to make adjustments or to stay where we are. If we do not change the circumstances that caused our situation in the first place, we are destined to re-cycle through our experiences. There are no social promotions. And as my mama always told me, "If you don't take care of yourself, no one else will." Our bodies are a temple, and nothing is more important than taking care of what God gave us—our body, mind, and spirit!

Whatever you've experienced, know that you can receive what God has for you. Live the victorious life, share your victories with others, and give Him praise for all things at all times!

I believe that we can be like the woman with the issue of blood. Her faith healed her. The words Jesus spoke to her are applicable today: *He said to her, "Daughter, your faith has healed you. Go in peace and be freed from your suffering."*

A Note from the Author

Thank you for joining me on this journey and for allowing me to share my story with you, a story that I never imagined telling. I never envisioned experiencing such a tremendous amount of pain. Often it takes unusual challenges to get our attention and to give us a capacity to empathize and minister to others.

I hope that by reading this, you understand that you are never alone. When you are in the midst of your struggles, many times you feel that no one knows what it's like to be in your situation. I have found through talking to many people that even though we may not talk about them, we all have issues and many of us are in warfare. Remember that one of the enemy's most effective tools is to make us believe we're in it all alone and that we must suffer in silence. We help ourselves and others as we share our struggles and our triumphs. You, my friend, are not alone.

I now understand what Paul meant when he said he knew what it was like to have plenty and not to have enough. I understand abundance and lack—not just in the material, but in the physical, emotional, and spiritual aspects of life. Having grown up in the church, I thought I understood what Christianity was all about, but now I truly understand what faith is. Through years of poor physical health and a traumatic marriage, I've come to understand the meaning of perseverance and the power of prayer.

A Journey Back to Me marks a whole new beginning of my life. I am ready to get on with the plan the Lord has for my life. His permissive will allowed some tough obstacles along the way, yet I still stand. As I look back over the journey, I realize He has always been there and provided my every need. I eagerly look forward to the next journey because I have a track record; I have gone through. I stated in the letter at the beginning of the book that I believed that the journey was in preparation for something. I know that when we endure through the obstacle course of life, our rewards await us at the end of the race.

I now look forward to the new life that awaits me. It is a new journey. It only gets better from here. I have new friends, a new love for life, and a fresh start on my career. I am regaining my passion for life and an appreciation for being renewed physically, emotionally, and spiritually. I believe I am ready for whatever may come. I have been conditioned to persevere. I know how to pray, wait, watch, and take action. I know who I am and whose I am. My destination is the abundant life. The next journey starts today.

As I move into this wonderful new journey, I confidently pass the baton on to you.

May He continue to bless you.

An Invitation to Salvation

To those of you who may not have a spiritual relationship with God, this journey may be His way of meeting you at this junction in your life. This could be your first step to discovering the essence of life. If you are not sure of your salvation or desire to begin your relationship with Him, please pray the prayer of salvation below. Be encouraged--your journey can begin today!

"For God so loved the world that he gave his one and only Son, that whoever believes in him shall not perish but have eternal life." —John 3:16

Dear Heavenly Father,

I invite you into my heart. I accept and believe John 3:16. I believe that Jesus Christ died and arose so that I could be saved today. I confess all my sins to you Lord and ask that you cleanse me. I ask for your forgiveness, knowing that you have already forgiven all my sins. Thank you for forgiving me and for blessing me in spite of what I have done in the past. I acknowledge my salvation and that I am beginning a new life. I give my life to you so that I may begin to live in a way that pleases you. My past is behind me and I walk into my future with you in my heart. Amen.

BIBLIOGRAPHY

Beattie, Melody *Codependent No More* (Center City, Minnesota: Hazelden Foundation, 1987, 1992).

Jones, Johnny *LIFE Support Leader's Handbook* (Nashville, Tennessee: LifeWay Press, 1993).

MacDonald, Gordan *Ordering Your Private World* (Nashville, Tennessee: Thomas Nelson Publishers, 1985).

Piper, Watty *The Little Engine That Could* (New York: Platt & Mark, 1930).

Turner, Tina with Kurt Loder. *I, TINA* (New York: Avon Books, 1987).

GRATITUDE

Thank you to the people who worked with me to make this book a reality:

Dawn Cherie Kennedy

Judy King

Henry Long

Debra Minor

Jacqueline Page

Larry Sachnowitz & his staff

Jennifer Agnew Scott

COMMUNICATE WITH CONSANDRA!

If you would like information about *A Journey Back to Me* products and services including:

•Speaking Engagements•
•Workshops•
•Conferences•
•Retreats•
•Inspirational Products•
•Coaching•
•Consulting•

You may contact her by writing:

ConSandra Jones
P.O. Box 542021-2021
Houston, Texas 77254
E-mail: cjbustr@aol.com
Website: www.consandrajones.com
Or call 713.334.0200

ORDER FORM

A Journey Back to Me

Code	Item	Description	Cost	Qty	Total
JBM	Book	A Journey Back to Me	$12.00		
JBMJJ	Daily Journal	A Journal of My Journey	$10.00		
WJ	Daily Journal	Wisdom for the Journey	$10.00		
				Subtotal	
			Texas residents add 8.25% tax		
		Shipping & Handling (add $3.00 + $1 for each additional item ordered)			
				Total	

COMPLETE AND MAIL TO: *KOINONIA Publishing,*
P.O. Box 542021, Houston, Texas 77254-2021

E-mail: cjbustr@aol.com
Website: www.consandrajones.com
To charge by phone, please call 713-334-0200.

Name _____

Address _____

City _____ State _____ Zip _____

Phone Number _____ Fax Number _____ E-Mail Address _____

□ Check □ VISA □ MasterCard □ Amex □ Discover □ Diners Club

Card # _____ Exp Date _____ Signature _____